Artists
and
Lovers

Artists
and
Lovers

Irina
Kuzminsky

Copyright

Edited by
Cover Image courtesy Shutterstock
Cover and Layout Design: W.S.D.G.

Dedication

…for all who have given themselves with passion to art and to love and for the artists of love and the lovers of art everywhere…

Table of Contents

Artists
and
Lovers

Lived Poetry

Strikes—the heart
Annuls—the mind
And opens—the soul's door
To song

Special Offer

Lady of the Labyrinth
Guarded by griffins
Sits by the water
Holding the double-edged
labyrinth key.
It's yours if you want it.
Today: special offer.

Free.

Kos

Kos

In the footsteps of statues we trod
And the ghost of a statue informed us.
In the footsteps of goddesses and heroes
We learned that standing and speaking were one.
How far did we need to go
Before our true voices spoke within us?

Many cracked pistachio nuts later our bodies
Gleamed in the white roughness of towels.

High in the mountains clarity confronted us.
Did the stones suffer to be pared to such austere nobility?
Carved by wind, sun and rain temples and trees stood firm.
Who wields the chisel which must work in living matter?
Stand and submit to the artist's blows.
What is left is needed. Refined to its truth.

Descending from revelations we watched the young in
tavernas,
Admiring the animal grace they confided in.
Yet their features were muddied through lack of the quests
of thought.

Ours was another way.

It led us through baptisms at water troughs
Ruins which spoke under a murderous sun
Crosses at roadsides marking death's passage.

It led us to taste the sweetness of figs amid deserted houses,
Crumbling, yet locked still against intruders.

It brought our bodies face to face,
Made simple through longing and thirst.

The land and the sky were not without mercy.

Olives and wine.
Honey and salt.
Bread and our juices.

The land was not without mercy.

In the whiteness of sheets and towels I welcomed
transparency.

On Patmos

Amidst rocks, beneath a sky of no mercy
You chose a cave and sought to people it.
Lambs, women, precious stones sparkled within.
Would they not sparkle brighter in the sun?

Black against whitewashed walls, a people
sought escape from the sun's power.
Sun kills, and you foretold us flames.

Bearing the sun's brunt, lurching on blue-black swell,
We came in torpor to your island, our bodies
protesting at so much denial.

With other sacrilegious pilgrims of a secular age
We looked in Chora
for the chora? For visions,
Revelations in the flesh.

Black crystallized no answer.
Truth, hard and white, bore down upon us
in laminated flames.

It was the sun that won.
We did not see what we had come for.

A Space

A wooden floor
A mirror filled with faces from past lives
whose presence flits across or watches
> half-indulgent
> half-impatient
A gallery
A door onto a garden and more walls
used by the cat for her majestic promenade
with which she teaches unaware
each movement's sleek and living grace
A string of bells
A board with arcane drawings traced in chalk
—These are the outlines of a space
> in which mysteriously
> Other spaces interlock.

You, teacher, move and measure and release
and help us carve the flow of time.
The light behind those eyes is also
light-
ness
of such mettle
it can flare against the deed
but not the doer
and disclose the needed
following the rhythms of the need
> And led on by your thread we trace
> the geometric dance of sacred forms
> engendering webs of our true selves.

Into the Snowstorm with Turner

You looked
so well and long
into the heart of things
There came a time
—as time must always come—
        while looking
when your painter's eye
became an eye
which could see further
into darkness
into light.

You painted what you saw
as things unveiled to you their patterns
and dared you glimpses of the spiral's heart
to plunge into the vertigo of waves, of wind and night.

Denuded now of all the cherubs
who peripheral adorn
full of baroque effrontery
your vortices

Greys, blacks, white sails reveal and revel in death's
        spiralling

But nothing could your visionary eyes
        —not dizziness, not dissipating ornament, nor even
        dissolution—
distract from vision
And having shown the order in demise
You take us further
into Sunrise and the reborn light.

Venice

variations and cadences

Some call you spectral, but not I,
Why blame you when the fault is mine
My flesh as yet too solid, well-defined,
Unblended with the limpid air
As are your land and water...
Bemirrored and bemasked
Reflecting and concealing
You point with laughing finger at your own and other selves
And show the apparency of all facades
which open out onto yet others...

Your senseless arches sensually mirror
arching bridges
And bathed in muted smiles and sighs
I float through you, the floating city—
Yet that is not enough, still not enough
For from the balustrades you challenge me:
Still lighter! Lighter! Learn to fly!—

I float past blues and pinks and greys
And tree-like chandeliers which flower into light.
Their light, your light conpenetrates with mine
and finds an inner flowering—

Lost and not lost I wander
among alleys and canals
silent and still
which then erupt in talk and jostling laughter
reclaimed as quickly by the alley's turn
and by the night...

With gentleness you sink into your beauty
Reflected in the glass of mirrors
draped in beads and blooms of glass—

The peeling paints and weeping plasters know
They, too, will be reclaimed—
They are the ornament of every building,
Speaking:

None.
None is, shall be exempt
from such immersion
Into seas of light.

Homage to Brancusi

Polished light
your surfaces
you polished
until light no other presence
and infinity
—would that my words
I'd polish
until light
no words

Into the Soapsuds

Throwing a word over your shoulder
to satisfy a question,
You casually dive into your mind,
Your fingers diving into dirty soapsuds—
Your words remain unauthored,
As unnamed as those artisans of stone
who carved their arabesques
and strangely poignant twisted faces
onto cathedral walls.
Your husband, lover, son goes off
with your few words (—said so in passing,
it might have been the water or the wind that spoke
them—)
to amass greater triumphs
clothed in which he returns to you
to spread his peacock's tail—

You will admire the plumage
And if I asked you now what you had said
Incredulous you'd smile,
for it was nothing, soon forgotten.

To an Unknown Woman Artist

Studiously poring over photos which
reach back into strata of prehistory
perhaps left better undisturbed
I come across your face or, rather,
Absence of your face.

You stand there, ill at ease among the others,
profile aquiline,
your bearing proud, aloof.
No family can claim you as its own
your actions scream
as photo after photo shows
your efforts at disfiguring your face.

Efface, efface all traces!

That one is not me,
the one holding a child's hand,
seated at a table,
midst other faces of one blood

(Not yours!)

Efface! Disfigure
what already in that setting
is disfigured.

Only your brushmarks still remain
And there, you show your face.

Picasso in Hong Kong

Buste de femme—Study for Demoiselles d'Avignon 1907

She's captured by the canvas
And would weep if she could
Eyes brim with sadness

Who has put me here?
And, more important,
Who will free me?
Who has imprisoned me
Behind black lines
with such nonchalant ease?

And, more important,
Who will now release me?

Buste de femme—Study for Demoiselles d'Avignon 1907

At least the other she had eyes
Not I
Brown lines are all I'm given

I'm blind—
No pupil to grant life
perhaps a window to a soul

I am reduced
To careless lines
To brown and cream

Perhaps the red splash on my forehead
Marks the place
Where his brush killed me

24   Irina Kuzminsky

Tête d'homme 1908/9

Tête d'homme 1908/9

Men's heads are better
—Are allowed a certain dignity
Their eyes closed in repose
They're noble, sentient
And though derivative of Africa
These masks
Are not devoid of strength
Nor of humanity

Nu couché 1908

Nu couché 1908

My body twists and turn in pain
      what are you doing?
I have no face...
My body twists and turns in pain
      what are you doing?
Where there was beauty
You have placed
An ugly twisted silent pain
Which screams itself to
hoarseness in a mouthless silent agony...

What are you doing?

      Irina Kuzminsky

Nude on white background 1927

Nude on white background 1927

Me—no—no me—
No recognition
A black crude line
Vagina mouth dentata
Abstracted of my essence
Abstracted from humanity
I am no longer woman
Just one used object for his line

The Sculptor 1931

The sculptor 1931

Bust
Statue
But I have revenge
I'm more alive than he
Who sculpted me
My eye sees me
Nose mouth and breasts
All present
—So see me
See me
I'm bird
I'm predator
I will consume him

La Femme au Stylet 1931

La femme au stylet 1931

Dismembered
Killed
Teethed
Ugliness
—Your own
—This is your anima
Your inside woman
How do you find her then?
And does she please you?
artist
painter
paul

Femme assise dans un fauteuil rouge 1932

Armchair and body
        are one
My head detaches
And attaches to the chair
With no link to my body
        —almost
My breasts are balls
Mouth—a blind eye
Has been denied
The power of speech
        and protest.

Dormeuse 1927

Dormeuse 1927

Feathery machine cogs for lashes
    and for mouth
In a grey sameness
    of disgust.

Femme à la collerette 1926

Femme à la collerette 1926

Reduced to nausea
Machine no body
Nothing but a thing

L'étreinte 1970

L'étreinte 1970

Your embrace was
Is
As bestial as you
My breast bleeds reds
For all you have denied me

Claude dessinant, Françoise et Paloma 1954

Claude dessinant, Françoise et Paloma 1954

My embrace mine
I shall protect
Protect them
Through my embrace
I'll care and save them
From you

Maternité 1971

Maternité 1971

You have my mouth
Its beauty
The rest imprisoned
In your strange contortions
But—this child will be safe
Though I am nothing to you
        but this line
This child is mine.

Irina Kuzminsky

Dormeuse aux persiennes 1936

Dormeuse aux persiennes 1936

My face spills out
        of me
Somewhere in there
My dreams
Maybe of love
But I know better
Now that I have met you

Tête d'homme barbu 1938

Tête d'homme barbu 1938

Bristling faun
With arrogance
Sharp pointy ears
And beard
Yet orange eyes
Speak sentience
And soul

L'enfant aux colombes 1943

L'enfant aux colombes 1943

The birds are pure
And have escaped
Your fantasies
Yes almost
One—distorted—sits uncomfortable
     on a chair
It would far rather fly from
The other perches
Sees the sky
And might well leave this frame

Yes
Birds are pure
Alone they have escaped you

Portrait de Marie Thérèse 1937

Portrait de Marie Thérèse 1937

Green gentleness
With blonde
    blue
    pink
I'm thoughtful here
You have not wiped
My fine intelligence
From this traced face
—but have allowed a grace
I had before I met you.

Portrait de Dora Maar 1937

Portrait de Dora Maar 1937

Green blue and red
I'm thinking—
Sad but not weeping
Not yet weeping
Although my eyelashes
Which you have drawn so big
Will fall soon with my tears

.   .   .

Why all this anger?

Why all this anger?
And wherefore the hate?
What Faustian bargain did you strike
To gain such fame?
And did it force you to destroy all beauty
Which might cross your path?
Alone the dove escaped—
And held a portion of your soul
Which thirsted still for beauty—
Why did you fear the woman so
You must destroy her?
Why did you sell your brush?
What price your soul?

Alone the dove took flight
But
Sorrowful
She could not save your soul.

The Dancer's Soul

And if I fall
the tangled web of words
insipid and banal
shall eat the dancer's soul
which speaks—not words withal—
but space-traced bodies' languages of flight

—But heavy, heavy is the plight
of human eyes and human mind and human soul
when words which label what the senses know
shroud over senses' knowing

Our senses atrophy in protest
—But concepts are the thing we're told
And labels count more than the thing itself
And butchered cows
and plaster casts of heaped up scraps
harsh wheezing screams
robotic motion
And lines which hold no deeper motive than themselves
Are full of subtlest meaning
—so we're told
And worthy of our senses' adoration
and the submission of our minds –

And if I fall
the tangled web of words
insipid and banal
shall eat the dancer's soul

Our dancers' souls must atrophy in protest
they ask for bread, are given stones
So on we smile, mouth words, debate the concepts
obey the powers which label
And marvel at the emperor's new clothes

So weep our dancers' souls
Our dancers' souls

    dancers

        souls

Chinese Whispers
- on viewing Chinese calligraphy in Beijing

Contemplation of the unknown
Distils into a presence
Of black on white
Strange writing opens pictures into meaning
But I remain bemused
And yet a horse shakes off the brushstrokes which have
       formed it
And gallops off the wall towards me
One moment of its joy
Is barely held—
An echo
On that wall

Words

An Imploration and an Invitation

Thus speaks Eve.

> Lilith,
> come to me as
> sister,
> And do not reject my
> strength.
> For I was not afraid
> to lose the mindless
> dream I led
> And release fear.
>
> Now help me—you
> in grandeur
> To see myself as
> strong
> And I will help in
> my turn
> you
> unlearn
> the bitter pleasure of
> instilling fear.
> Together we
> must walk
> And claim again the
> holy garden as our own.

Thus speaks Eve.

Marrying the Mysteries

Marrying the Mysteries
Time—upon—Time
Mistress, Mage and Merging
—Stepping out of Line
Thought I had no Learning
But the Steps ring true
Summoned from Caves' Whispering
Body Spirit through
The Maze—Leaps
Through the glass—flies
Through the mirror—passes
As Soul.

Maternal Embrace
- after a modern Chinese painting seen in Beijing -

The child
Enveloped in the body of the mother
Held tight content

Oh she would keep you safe forever
    If she could
Within the confines of her body

Madonna-like inclines her head
In recognition of the fact
That even she—
Cannot.

Sister of Isis

You walked on fingertips of ice through darkness
A stifled darkness into which you came to see
If marriage bones, dis-membered in the darkness
Could, pieced together, light again your memory.

That in your search you might be unimpeded
You let the brightness of your features be eclipsed,
Their darkness melting gently into darkness
You coursed in muffled flight through land and sea.

Your shadow, darker than the darkness,
Fell cooling on the burning heavy dust,
But burning was all men desired now
And cooling moisture made them clammy with disgust.

Here was a gift to which they had grown unaccustomed
And credited your shadow with a vulture's claws;
You were the mare which rode them to their nightmares,
Yours was the shrillest harpy's voice.

Disturbed they said you were the black disturbance,
Black fallen angel, snatcher of their children's lives.
They muttered midst themselves and plotted better
          weapons
And carefully locked up their wives.

Meanwhile you wrapped yourself still further into darkness
Slid into cores of rocks and lava flows and wells,
Your mission—to re-member in the darkness
The sickened light you could again make well.

The Judas Kiss

I know. I am known.
I see. I am seen.
I trust. I am betrayed.

A judas Kiss
Full on the mouth
A passionate embrace
You—lover
Thought you'd sell me down the river
Body money slave
Judas!
Who gave you words and gesture
And how can I escape
To hate you
Who brought to me my death
Deep trust seeds deep betrayal
Judas—my lover
Full on the mouth
Your kiss
Who drank my milk
And at my banquet feasted

Full on the mouth
You kiss
Not another
Betray
not another
Than—
You
—Judas, my lover
Brought resurrection
          to me.

But, my dark lover,
Who'll grant you that
judas kiss?

An Unkept Promise

.... Let us follow in the footsteps of your mindfulness
Image of the East and Image of the West ....

No words
Just wild wild colours painted in the sky
By an uneducated god
Emissions of an orgasm
Spilling over into oranges and golds and pinks and reds

It's from the time
When Shiva opened his third eye
(Amazed an energy should equal his)
And beheld Parvati and love

Beloved!
I drink deep into dark eyes
And know this truth
That God and Goddess *are*
forever
irrevocably in love...

And as we quest to link our cultures and our colours
     and our creeds
The god and goddess in us
Will not be denied
And they span space, make loops in time
From fullness come and fullness give
And full remain
To forge our mythic lives.

* * *

Our bodies
Touching thrashing in the sacred dance
Awaken to a deeper knowing than our conscious minds
In them encoded all we need to know
And with the touch of fingers, ears and eyes
The memories return
Of how we danced in other times
And slowly slowly knowledge comes
Until we see each other naked face to face
And nothing comes now to disturb this empty space
As with your wand of light
You enter sacred space
And light the darkness from within
There to unfurl illusions of atoms...

* * *

Pure longing flows toward no goal
And pure desire knows no fulfilment
Beloved! Only when I overflow
Is giving free and gives you freedom.

* * *

I am reflected through the prism of consciousness in you
You are reflected through the prism of consciousness in me
The surface plays and crackles
What pool is still enough to show your depths to you?
My surface breaks and ripples
So stiller still when you approach me
Don't throw any stones
To cause more turbulence and patterns
For in the depths of two still pools
These eyes
You'll see your image
As it plays and glitters.

* * *

Beloved! Can't you see?
In granting sovereignty to me
All you desire will come to be.

* * *

Whenever darkness chooses to ignite
Light—please believe me—
Brighter glows
Together let's remove the veil
To glimpse such brightness
That our dazzled eyes can only darkness see
And in that seeing intimately know
Black wisdom's light
Desireless passion

* * *

A knife wound in the belly
—Our parting—
An animal screams
—Somewhere inside—
Obsession
—roving, dreaming and desiring
Hours stretching to eternity
While you, my wounded lover,
Are more present
in this seeming absence of your form
Than in your presence.

* * *

You say my tears will weep you dry
My friend what is it makes you try
So very hard to make me cry?

* * *

Psyche speaks

Psyche speaks

I saw the god in you beloved
And I cannot help
But that I see him still
Although it seems to me
You'd sometimes rather
I had nothing seen.
And—if I light my lamp
And—caught by beauty
Drip hot oil onto your face
Please—do not fear me
Do not go
For I have seen
The golden radiance of you
Until my heart aches with the memory of glory
And I still maintain
This face of glory is indeed your Face.

* * *

Thus in abandonment
I was surprised by light
And this immensity
My silence plumbs
And finds no bottom...
In shipwreck
I was found by depth
And dying dying
while I could not die
I knew
        that I did live
Only
        so I could die

* * *

Beloved! Masks and faces
Labourer and king
A warrior's strength
A sage's knowing
And a fool's despair
Conspire to tarnish and conceal
The empty untamed truth
Of freedom.

* * *

There are but waves
There is but space
Together we
Make waves in space
Which soon enough subside
So we can rest.

Keats' agonia

Full full of sorrow hangs the house's air
Full full of pain and sorrow at death's coming

> *Come I to thee and thou to me*
> *Perhaps we shall cheat sorrow*
> *Yet she who comes*
> *In beauty comes*
> *Is la belle dame who's sans merci*

Youth who sang beauty's pains and truths
And proved ephemeral as beauty's passing
Who eked out days of bleeding semi-starved
And dreamed sometimes of farewelled love

> *Come I to thee and thou to me*
> *Perhaps we shall cheat sorrow*
> *Yet she who comes*
> *In beauty comes*
> *Is la belle dame who's sans merci*

Hair's flowing fineness and a poet's grace
Unsuited to the faithlessness of others' ways
A living spirit touched by purity's ideal
He asked in death for shrouds of violets

> *Come I to thee and thou to me*
> *Perhaps we shall cheat sorrow*
> *She came to thee*
> *She took your breath*
> *La belle dame sans merci*

Soon, torment over, he was dead
The house's air hangs still full full of sorrow
The shroud of violets masks the sweet smell of decay
Perhaps it cheats the sorrow

She came for thee
She took your breath
She took your breath away
For she who comes
In beauty comes
Is la belle dame
And she is sans merci

The Dancer

"The whole world is but fire and oblation."

The rhythms her body traced
Were Air's oblations,
Filaments of light, could they be fixed—
Ephemeral
Untorn
Unlike her body
Torn, strained, aching
An oblation to the dance.

—Yet that comes later.
First the book is written—in the air
Then sacrificed
—Like holy Taoist Writs
Thrown into fire
To feed the fire's embrace.
Just so her body is consumed
And offered as a holocaust to grace.

There's No Surrender

There's no surrender to despair
Just this quiet listening to sorrow
There's no succumbing to fear's rage
Just this quiet speaking which lends grace
To speaker listener alike
So long as speech is twinned with right
So long as truth is not dismayed
So long as wisdom dawns—perchance—
In one more meeting one more gaze
Of eyes which listen and which say—
There is no fear which undoes grace
There is no hurt which love can't heal
There is no barrier beyond compassion's reach.

An Icon of the Dormition

You lie
Bejewelled mermaid
In death becalmed
Your body floats within the waters of the womb
Eyes closed
Hands folded

You lie
Bejewelled by the halo of your life
As if this slumber were indeed a death
As though the waters of your womb could drown you
What latent power upon these waters is afloat
Eyes closed
Hands folded

You lie
A pose
This beautiful repose
Suspended between sun and earth in potency
The singularity:
This threshold of your passing
Through the waters of your birth
Eyes closed
Hands folded

Pietà

Pietà

I am the mother of my father
and the sister of my husband,
and he is my offspring.
The Thunder, Perfect Mind

Just as God
carved them
Mary
Jesus
out of Light

Deep memory
The sculptor's
Causes us to see
His body raised up into Hers
So that in Death
A Resurrection once again occurs
The Son becomes One
With the Mother
As before the Origin of things
The Mother raises Him into Herself
And in this Marriage
Melded
They arise again
With knowledge of the Light—

Gestures of Sumer

One hand is raised to lips
To cover them
His other pointing down
In admiration and in awe
Before the holy revelation
As she draws back the sacred veil
To show the holy triangle
Whence all creation comes.

. . .

The goddess and the god
With steady gait approach
And there—between them—
Dwarfed
A woman holy in her nakedness

. . .

There is another
Central to the seal
We see her in the act of drawing back her veil
To bless the gathering
With a most sacred sight—
Her body.

. . .

Lady of the Beasts

Naked and winged
All straight lines and angles
She stands
Lithe as a gazelle
Amongst them.

• • •

The priestesses make offerings to writhing scorpions
Whilst she, the goddess, watches—
Spare us the scorpion's sting
Spare us the harsh and waterless desert
Spare us death.

• • •

The god's feet rest upon the bull
Mighty is the bull of Uruk
While the goddess intercedes
And leads a man
Into the holy presence.

The Magdalens

Magdalen penitent
Upon her knees
Red hair cascading to reveal a curve of breasts

Should it not rather be the painters
Penitent
For using her for their great sanctioned pleasure?

Yet even in such guise
Her image burned with brightness
And she lived on in furtive fantasies of pleasure

Thus unforgotten though maligned
She waited patiently
Until her time would come.

Eternity

Eternity had come to call
It waited patiently outside
While you stood still looked at the door
Not knowing what you should decide

Eternity's too big an ask
A risky enterprise
It changes everything—or could—
Do I could I—you think I should—
Open the door and peer outside?

The fear of empty spaces bites
Your calling's for a nice warm den
So what if when you're at full height
You can't quite stand? That is no sin!

Far safer then, to stay inside
Far more secure to lock the door
But with some luck and Eve's first bite
Pandora's curiosity (—or thirst for knowledge—)
Might
Just might win through.

Brinkmanship

There is a way of sitting at the brink
—Of Prophecy?—of Fallacy?
And hearing wheels rotating as they pass
—sweet Chariots of light you never enter
Hard as you run—They fly
Until you only glance out sitting on a sill
—as they pass by.
This brinkful I have drunk of
By the beaker
Poured by a leaky sky
While life stared at me through the open window
And while I—poised on the brink—
Could not decide to Prophesy.

● ● ●

Bridging space I hanker for withdrawal.
On the brink of flowering
The pull of closure strengthens.

● ● ●

What nourishment could now sustain
a wingful's flight—
When there is pain—too much of Pain—
In having to stand still—and fight.

They

The shell-shocked passengers of night are steadfast.
They wait, half-dazed, upon the coming of the morn.
With grimy wings the carriers of the light begin to trespass
Upon the smog-filled territory of the ones whose province
        is to mourn.
They will not fail—although their feathers fragile seem
They will not fall—their wing frames are of tempered steel
Their eyes seem cold yet ready to ignite
A passion which is born of bearing witness to a long cold
        night.
Too weary now to suffer, too abused to fear
Desires slip through their mouths and words dispassionate
        appear.
Yet Passion is their knowing
Just as Passion is their right
That Passion born of burning
Through frozen wastes of might
Lost to despair
Their eyes
Bear Passion
With and For.

They're weary shell-shocked steadfast
They know what they're waiting for.

Narcissus

Narcissus
Narcissus
You stare at
Your screen
These words and—these pictures—
can't lie
You're perfect—so friended
At least half-divine
Your image—is flawless
And that's taken time.

The screen doesn't sleep
Machines never tire
Relentless they prod you awake
Your image absorbs you
You are self-defined
And nothing can touch you on line.

Narcissus
Narcissus
Reality sucks
Sink into the mirror
And see
Perfection reflecting
And whispering—you're free
Of messy reality.

The screen smirks and flatters
It sucks in your gaze
Your beauty astounds it
You love what it says
You don't need another

You're intimate now
You're intimate now you're on line

Narcissus
Narcissus
Illusion is best
You're drowning
You can't look away
You cannot forget
It's got in your head
There's no one can reach you in time.

The Left Hand Spiral

Against the sun the earth spins round
Against the sun the moon revolves
Against the sun our helix spirals tightly wound
Against the sun the Milky Way evolves.

The left hand spiral is creation's path
The left hand spiral brings the galaxies to be
The left hand spiral dreams creation into life
The left hand spiral is the woman's path.

So let us circle sisters, linked, against the sun
And let us dream our conscious dreams to life
And let us see with womb eyes what must yet be born
And let us bring this consciousness to light.

the red streak fades on the horizon

the red streak fades on the horizon
sends orisons to sky and sea
while seagulls blackened
by the sun's demise
salute red endings on the wing
and all the while fierce tenderness arises
in waves and billows
from the birthing sea.

thus slowly simply sense awakens
stroked into being by the rhythmic sea.

The Dakini to Her Partner

I have drunk of the nectar of your lips
I have felt your image in my heart
My cells have vibrated with yours
You awaken longing in me
For a union so intense and complete
It will transform us both.
As the dark is illumined with your consciousness
As my energy flows in rhythm with yours
So are we entrained into the place
Of our power and our compassion
Flying into the sky through this meeting
With me and with you.

Man with Your Wild Wild Celtic Heart

... for J

Man with your wild wild Celtic heart
Who seeks the Word's abundance
He delights in—
And overflows with words and gifts of Self for all who
come—
And yet you fear your giving falls into the Void
But this Void welcomes and receives and then becomes
The cauldron She has now prepared for your renewal
From which pour riches, ecstasy and heady wine
Until your head is quenched
And deeper wisdom starts to flow
From that sweet river centred in your core
And you yourself begin to soar
Not only in your fecund mind
But in your whole and holy heart

Man with your Celtic wild wild heart

Thus shall She call you poet and the Source's bard

And you shall sing—
No more bereft of Euridyce.

Orpheus Sings

Melodies rise to the rim of the glass
>Frothing
>Waiting

This drunkard's lips crave the solace they bring
>Trembling
>Aching

Drink deep and deeper and froth at the mouth
>Exulting
>In frenzy

Lips touching lips drinking wine into song
>Hear me
>Taste me

Orpheus sings now his head free of hopes
>Praising
>Lamenting

Star dazzled eyes stare as galaxies float
>Promised
>Assuaging

Gutters flush roses as his head floats by
>Singing
>Blazing

Eye sockets stare and my arteries pulse
>Burning
>Dancing

Spirit sears throat birthing song birthing sound
>The Word
>Is waiting

Secrets of Azrael

Fierce eyes
Implacable and stern
Your upright presence
Fierce eyes
Implacable they burn
Your stern presence

Signals Death.

———

Angel of endings
Approach approach
With wings which don't emit a whisper
No hum
No wisp of rustling
To announce your coming

Angel of fierce fulfilment
And fiercer stillness
I sense your presence

Approach.

———

Clarion call of silence
Your gaze
Gazing
Your gaze
Upon me
As I arise
Summoned in silence
Air swirls
Leaves no bearings
Yet I can't falter
Steady your gaze
Gazing
Upholds me
Arisen
Angel of endings
Transport me
Through your approaching
Which draws me
Deep into your arms.

———

No rustle
As your wings enfold me
Fierce eyes burn like embers
Like coals
Clarion call
Your gaze
Gazing
Upon me enfolded
Silence is pregnant
—No sound.

———

Angel of Death
Enfold me
Stern cold your gaze
Burn through me
Power of endings
Uphold me
Dark Lover—
Come!

———

Blackness swirls
Coal embers burn
Steady your gaze
Holds me in embrace
Succumb!

Gentle and fierce
Overcome
I am
Held and embraced
In your gaze
Rivers of gold molten flow
Flowing through me
Deep from earth's bounty
This grace

Know
This ore
Is molten
Is gold.

———

Angel of endings
There at each beginning
Primeval fire
Life's grace
Eagle of powers
Flight cloaked in silence
Bears power through dark to
This place
Angel of mysteries
Come to transform me
Clarion call
Your gaze
Darkness is swirling
Phoenix arising
Burn through the void
Its face
Waves ripple patterns
Music exciting
Silence's womb
Births love's trace.

———

Surrender

Possession! Permeate and come
You golden river flanked by scarlet banks
I'm taken taken shaken
Through to my very core
I am cast down and ripped apart
Awakened
I am undone and worshipping
And desperately taken
I am adoring and convulsed
And tremblingly possessed
I'm welcoming I'm open
And intangibly I'm blessed
By this strange visitation
Crashing oceans through my ears
And forcing my blood's coursing
Through my arteries and veins
I am possessed and shaken
Through to my very core
When this force takes and throws me
Flings me down onto the floor
I am exceeded superseded
And undone
I am extended and transcended
And I run
Into the arms of golden fire
Where I relive
The memory of time and worlds conceived
And flung about
I rise
And shaken more and more
I feel the serpent rising
Hissing kisses up my core

Immobile
Standing
Smiling
fall laugh risen
rise fall soar.

Possessed by Aphrodite

These mirrors now convey
A glamour which can steal upon me
When I have been a canvas
For the one who brings and takes delight

For I have been possessed,
Possessed by Aphrodite
Who's driven into rapture
By a curve, a voice, a tress of hair, a smile

All these she takes delight in
And steals upon to rapture
So she can know delight—again
Within the circle of a lover's arms

Yet say it was no goddess
But a nymph of flowers
When you yourself know likewise
That you too have been possessed,

Possessed by Aphrodite
And had the mirror tell you
You are the canvas for her charms.

The Teardrop of the Taj

(... after Tagore)

Grief turns to marble in the pleasant purgatory of the Taj
Suspended like a filigree of sadness from the sky
Who would have thought a living tear could set in stone
Infusing into perfect form a pain which was beyond
            enduring?

And they, the Lovers, are they caught still in this mourning?

Do they still rise to hear the music of the streams
So often dry now yet still held in memory's ears?
Or do their shadows search the grounds for promised fruits
And find expanses filled with levelled grass and too few
            birds?
And are these subjects—all the multitudes who mill around
      their tomb—
And do they watch, bemused, that so many should come...
Then, tiring, flee to their dark sanctuary below
Awaiting silence and the cool light of the moon
When they can stroll at peace at last through garden paths?

Was this the Paradise they sought while lying clasped into
            each other's arms?

Or—have they fled this cage of beauty and repose
Heeding the summons of the morning and the sun
To wander free at last through clouds and starlit paths
Hand held in hand
Each moment born anew
To rediscover in that moment
Paradise?

My Feet

My feet have skipped through pools of light
To splash through puddles
And stumble on through grief and joy
Past rocks and springy meadows
Brush flowers along the way
And tread on flowers when stung
Be caked in mud, washed clean in streams
Sink into quicksand, find firm ground
Thrill to the firewalk, find the water's path
Be pierced be soothed and dangle

My feet have splashed through puddles
To come home to pools of light...

The Poet's Breath

The poet's breath
Breathes in the web of earth
Distils its essence into words
Which point beyond and shift in meaning
Like shifting sands
Like spiders' webs
So strong so fragile—words
Will dance meaning over an abyss
     of forms and patterns constantly remade
        dissolved and then rewoven
Light has coagulated into denseness
To make the contours of your face
And light itself will shift these contours and unmake them—
—Yet—
The poet's breath breathes in this shifting web
And exhales words in open weave
Which let light through
And point beyond their meaning.

A Woman's Language

I roll the words round in my mouth
To taste them better
They say they now can tell
If it's a woman or a man
Who writes these words
I say, no need for calculations
I'll tell you now up front
I am a woman.
And I write.
And writing seek the words which will have taste and power
       to ensoul
And bathe the brain in all the senses.

Seems I was right.
There could be such a thing.
A woman's language.
Our syntax even—
That betrays our sex.
Computer programmes prove it, after all.
So gingerly, kid gloves on
My Oxford thesis spoke of this.
'Écriture féminine'.
The 'language of women'.
And then—thesis completed,
I, as a woman poet,
Claimed it.

Notes

p.17 *Into the Snow Storm with Turner* was inspired by one of Turner's greatest late paintings, **"Snow Storm" 1842**, depicting a steam boat in a storm. Turner claimed to have been lashed to the mast for four hours in order to observe this scene.

p.20 *Homage to Brancusi* was inspired by the gleaming polished surfaces of many of Brancusi's sculptures, particularly his abstract birds.

p.22 *To an Unknown Woman Artist* is based on fact – this particular woman artist did indeed systematically go through family photo albums and erase her face.

p.23 *Picasso in Hong Kong* was written after seeing an extensive Picasso exhibition at the Hong Kong Heritage Museum in 2012.

p.37 *The Dancer's Soul* was sparked by certain exhibits at the Tate Modern including those by Damien Hirst and other installations.

p.39 *Chinese Whispers* was inspired by a remarkable pen and ink drawing of a horse alongside calligraphy which I saw at the National Art Museum of China in Beijing. It was executed in the traditional classical Chinese manner by a twentieth century artist.

p.42 *Maternal Embrace* is based on a fine contemporary painting seen in an exhibition of modern art at the National Art Museum of China in Beijing.

p.53 *Keats' agonia* was written after visiting the Keats-Shelley Museum in Rome, the house next to the Spanish steps where Keats breathed his last succumbing to TB. *La belle dame sans merci* is of course one of Keats' most famous poems.

p.55 *The Dancer* – the quotation is from the Upanishads.

p.57 *An Icon of the Dormition* is inspired by a beautiful 17th century Russian icon of the Dormition of the Theotokos.

p.58 The starting point for *Pietà* were Michelangelo's sculptures, particularly his last unfinished Pietà currently in Milan. *The Thunder, Perfect Mind* is one of the texts recovered in the discovery of the Nag Hammadi Library.

.p. 59 *Gestures of Sumer* – I have always been fascinated by the ancient cylindrical seals of Sumer, so tiny and yet with such a wealth of detail on their surfaces, and the window they cast on a different world. These particular seals are held by the Morgan Library and Museum in New York.

p.61 *The Magdalens* arose from the many, very many paintings throughout Western art history which portray Mary Magdalene as a repentant prostitute.

p.70 *Man with Your Wild Wild Celtic Heart* is dedicated to a great contemporary poet, Jay Ramsay, in homage to his sense of mission and a life dedicated to fulfilling it.

p.71 *Orpheus Sings* is based on the myth of Orpheus, the archetypal musician and singer, who could move the trees and animals and stones themselves to dance by his music, and whose body is torn apart by the Maenads (followers of Dionysus) in Thrace but whose head continues to sing as it floats down the river.

p.72 *Secrets of Azrael*. Azrael, Thanatos, Eros, all lead to transformation. Azrael is most often known as the Angel of Death, though his name may also signify Help from God. In some traditions the number of his eyes is said to be the same as the number of people on earth.

p.79 *The Teardrop of the Taj* was inspired by the Taj Mahal, its famous love story, and Rabindranath Tagore's description of it as a 'teardrop'.

p.82 *A Woman's Language* is a tongue in cheek reference to my Oxford doctoral thesis which was indeed on 'écriture féminine' or the 'language of women'. A computer programme has now been developed which purports to tell you error free whether the writer is a woman or a man.

Acknowledgements

Into the Snowstorm with Turner was first published in *Acumen*.

Thus in abandonment (from *An Unkept Promise*) was first published in
light muses.

The following poems have all been set to music and have
appeared on three of my CDs:

Pure longing, Psyche speaks and *There are but waves* (all from *An Unkept
Promise*) appear on the CD *Would That I Could*.

The Dancer's Soul, Words (renamed *Lilith*) and *The Left Hand Spiral*
(renamed *Against the Sun*) all appear on the CD Roads *Travelled* by
Irinushka, while *Orpheus Sings* is on the CD *Orpheus Sings* by
Irinushka.

A big thank you to Kermit E. Heartsong for daring to believe
that a publisher can still make a difference to the world.

Bio

Irina Kuzminsky has spent her life on a quest for the feminine face of God. Living the quest through poetry, dance and music has been her life's work. Her academic background includes a scholarship to Oxford where she wrote her doctorate on the 'Language of Women' and was elected Junior Research Fellow in Humanities. Poetry publications include *Dancing with Dark Goddesses, light muses* (with artist Jan Delaney), *Contemplations, Into the Silence*, and poems in *Diamond Cutters* and *Soul of the Earth*. As Irinushka she has released three CDs of her poems set to music, *Would That I Could, Roads Travelled* and *Orpheus Sings*. Irina has performed her one woman dance, poetry and music show *Dancing with Dark Goddesses* in the UK, Germany, US and Australia.

Artists
and
Lovers

Irina
Kuzminsky

www.ingramcontent.com/pod-product-compliance
Lightning Source LLC
Chambersburg PA
CBHW071847090426
42811CB00035B/2350/J